PRAISE FOR

If the World Is Running Out

"Sometimes from the hot core of a poem a whole novel of warmth and wit may seem to radiate: this happens over and over in Kate Green's *If the World is Running Out*. These are poems from the center of a woman's life, deeply felt and intensely recorded. I enjoyed and admired this book."

—*Mona Van Duyn*

"Kate Green's narrative poems are confidently female, purposeful, lively, and are often quickened with wry humor. She tells us about her life as a white woman married to a black man; about the birth of her children; about her mother, and her mother-in-law. None of this is banal. All of it shines as brand-new as truth can, when back-lighted by insight."

—*Maxine Kumin*

"It's hard to say what has prompted the easy but certain authority of these poems, the exactitude of the images, the range of concerns, the wisdom and relish of the humor, the acquiescence to the past. Whatever has empowered her, Kate Green has found not simply 'a voice,' as the saying usually goes, but an ear for the voices of others who would sing. And she can sing."

—*Patricia Hampl*

TOURIST
IN THE
PURE
LAND

POEMS BY
Kate Green

HOLY COW! PRESS :: DULUTH, MINNESOTA :: 2014

Cover painting, "Skyscape–New Mexico 2005," acrylic on canvas,
by Kathy Gilbert (Pittsburgh, PA).

Author photograph by the The Photographers Guild (Saint Paul, MN).

Book and cover design by Anton Khodakovsky.

Printed and bound in the United States of America.

First printing, 2014

ISBN 978-0-9859818-4-6

10 9 8 7 6 5 4 3 2 1

The poem "Zen Deathbed Poems" is based on the book *Japanese Death Poems: Written by Zen Monks and Haiku Poets on the Verge of Death* by Yoel Hoffmann (Compiler, Introduction). North Clarendon, Vermont: Tuttle Publishing, 1998.

Grateful acknowledgement is made to The Bush Foundation for granting me two Artist Fellowships in Poetry. This provided me with the gift of open time and travel in which to find my tourist muse and write. Also, a deep thank you to the Loft Literary Center, Minneapolis, Minnesota for a Loft Mentor Award and a Loft McKnight Award which gave me time, support, and confidence during years when I was swamped with children. My heartfelt appreciation goes to painter and artist Kathy Gilbert for the use of her beautiful painting which graces the cover of this book. Thanks also go out to my publisher, Jim Perlman of Holy Cow! Press, for still supporting my poetry quest for over 30 years and for his unequaled patience.

This project is supported in part by grant awards from the Ben and Jeanne Overman Charitable Trust, the Elmer L. and Eleanor J. Andersen Foundation, the Cy and Paula DeCosse Fund of the Minneapolis Foundation, The Lenfestey Family Foundation, and by gifts from individual donors.

HOLY COW! PRESS books are distributed to the trade by Consortium Book Sales & Distribution, c/o Perseus Distribution, 210 American Drive, Jackson, TN 38301.

For inquiries, please write to:
HOLY COW! PRESS,
Post Office Box 3170, Mount Royal Station,
Duluth, MN 55803.

Visit *www.holycowpress.org*

This book is dedicated to
CARY WATERMAN,

earth traveler, poet and essayist,
"sister" goddess, mentor, and deep friend

"Neither the pure land nor hell exists outside ourselves; both lie within our own hearts. Awakened to this truth, one is called a Buddha; deluded about it, one is called a common mortal. The Lotus Sutra reveals this truth, and one who embraces the Lotus Sutra will realize that hell is itself the Land of Tranquil Light."

—Respectfully, Nichiren Daishonin, (1222–1282), from "Hell is the Land of Tranquil Light," *Soka Gakkai International*

TABLE OF CONTENTS

I

SAINTS AND FISHING

MOVIES

What I remember is being dropped off
in the rain in front of the neon
marquee of *The World* with two dollars
in my pocket and posters
of Rock Hudson and Peter Pan pasted
on the cement wall.
Inside I traded a ticket for a torn stub
I'd roll in my fingers as the lights
went dim and the stars in the ceiling
rolled their rhythm across the fake blue
curve of sky. Mildewed curtains
spread apart, a sea of faded red.
The cracked screen blinked into color,
scratchy soundtrack revving once,
then dying in a swoon through catcalls
of bands of bad kids in the balcony
who shredded popcorn boxes and heaved them
toward the earth of the first floor.
I held in my lap my cache
of Bit O' Honey, popcorn, and Junior Mints,
one hand in a cardboard box. I licked the salt
from a paper cut. Coke bottles
clinked down the slant of aisle
as I leaned into the ripped velvet seat
against the broken armrest.
The lion tilted his head and roared
or that blue queen of clouds,

the Columbia angel, rose
while spotlights crossed heavenward
over our plain lives.
Then came the dream of it, full as love
had been promised and in the blank dark
where all individual lives became faceless
backs of heads, we disappeared
into your mouths: Jack Lemmon,
Marilyn Monroe, Pinocchio.
In the reflected light of your illusion
there was nothing in our lives
we could not forget.

THE FUNCTION OF MEMORY

When your eyes cease to contain
the violet bougainvillea of the winter vacation,
the flower does not abandon you.
Nor the coral cabins, nor the weathered man
fishing solitary by the Gulf.
These things will never leave you.
Without loss there is no singing
of palm fronds rattling in unexpected rain
outside the open door of our motel.
No aching of the old café, La Bodega,
where my friend and I sat loving blue tables,
where canaries went wild
sensing the approaching storm.
We can't hold what we love,
in arms, in any way.
Can't hold them in until
they're pressed to us unchanging.
We cannot own the ripening fruit,
no single cloud, nor tropical rain
driving into salty ground.
That is why the gods have given us this gift
where all that is good settles in back of the eye
with tender hurt of a lover one has left
and left forever. All that is wrong,
the ordinary pain of marriage,
empty winter days, these also remain
but we touch them now more easily being gone.

I imagine memory is a slow act
of dying. Every moment we give up
the green view from the open door.
Every moment enter the rain.

BROOM

I sweep dust balls.
Ride across the room
on my kitchen broom.
I stir black animals
in acid. I feed children
candy. Several lifetimes,
I was burned
for not sweeping
perfectly enough,
for straw left on linoleum.
A tag of rag on the sink.
Sand at the bottom
of the pail. Now I clean
only my mind,
that webbed root cellar
of stored beets, carrots,
onions that rot in dirt.
Spider-spit patterns
hung in unseen corners.
Which jar holds nutrient?
Which poison?
The earth is cool.
Damp as a grave.
I am alive
down here.
I feed you.

Hunting

My father had a red checkered wool jacket like Paul Bunyan, a shotgun with shiny polished mahogany wood grain. I was afraid of it, stored on a high shelf in the hall closet over the hangers. After Uncle George taught me to shoot on summer vacation out in Colorado, I wasn't afraid of my father's gun. Uncle George made it fun, plus it was the west and we were cowboys. Not girls. Beer cans sat on the wood rail fence. Silver flash sunlight, big hairy arms around me, how the gun should go against my shoulder bone. Now sight down the barrel to the notch point. Arms shaky, then okay, bull's-eye. I wanted to win, not lose in front of my brother who'd gotten to go hunting last year with Dad, but we girls didn't. Took aim. Crack of the shotgun split my shoulder, banged in my brain, but I was all right.

The next year Dad let me go with him, grouse hunting. Old enough now, and with Uncle George's blessing. But I followed Dad too closely in the woods, and a birch branch swung back at me, whipping across my eye. I wore a patch for a week, proud of my injury. I didn't see a grouse. My injury was my trophy.

Now Dad has gone out to South Dakota hunting with some dads from the neighborhood. He'll be back late. I have to go to bed. When I wake up, I know he's back. Two beautiful pheasant feathers tacked to the bulletin board above my bed, right by the newspaper clipping of Khrushchev pounding his shoe on the table at the UN. I'd cut it out for our social studies unit and for some reason he fascinated me, as if there could be one single enemy. As if you could be safe hiding from that enemy by crouching under your metal school desk when the nuclear bomb test sirens went off. Be sure to cover your head, they told us. Iridescent feathers, long, blue-streaked. My parents had a game dinner. I didn't want to taste the bird.

GRACE

I stole the light-up-in-the-dark cross
from my friend in 4th grade
and hung it in my closet.
I'd go in and close the sliding door
among the Keds and brick-red sensible oxfords
my mother made me get instead of the black
patent-leather shoes with straps she'd never splurge for.
Standing there in the smell of ironed dresses,
I'd squint my eyes at the pale green plastic glow.
I had to hide from my family my search
for light absorbed into the thing that hung
right next to my nightgown on a hook,
my hands pressed together, split slices of bread.
"Why was so much killing done
in the name of Christ?" my mother asked at dinner
over fish sticks and peas.
"Why the Inquisition? The Crusades?"
I hid the cross under my bathrobe.
I'd go to the closet and touch it.
If I didn't hold it freshly to a light bulb,
it wouldn't glow at all or only faintly.
It didn't glow. Not much. Then faded
where I stood behind the ghosts of my school clothes.
I was not given grace easily with a name or an object.
The cross I'd stolen shone among the shoes
I didn't want. Grace was there but not as I pictured it.
It never is.

VACATION

Emptied out.
That's what you want.
Sea defined
by two rock islands
framing blue before blue
was a word.
But desire is not emptied out
and neither is the world,
fullness beyond embrace.
You cannot hold its pleasure
in your knotted heart
but it holds you.

KEY WEST: TENNESSEE WILLIAM'S HOUSE

That night we rode bikes along the Gulf of Mexico
on the blacktop road in salt wind, past the Holiday Inn,
the small pensioni and Bed and Breakfasts,
away from that cheap flop-house of a motel
you'd gotten us reservations at: Sea Paradise.
That afternoon we'd been to Ernest Hemingway's house,
taken the tour with that fabulous queen and we were
the only ones in the tour group who loved him.
And loved the weight of heat in the palm yard
where Ernest drank and struggled with the words,
but I thought, At least he had a wife. A writer needs
a wife, especially a woman writer. We rode out
and turned in the neighborhood streets, past
bougainvillea, and came finally on Tennessee William's house.
He was recently dead. We stopped in silence,
your long brown legs in blue shorts. You turned to me,
palmed your hair and said, "We'll always be lonely."
I knew it was true but just then I wasn't. I held
the rusty bike between my thighs and stared
at the white lattice fence in the darkness.

GARDEN

This garden I've ignored, I love as no other,
more than the one I fertilized with sheep manure,
blood meal, lime,
more than the one I fussed over, weeding obsessive rows.

This is the one I care about – monstrous comfrey
sprawled in the corner, grapevine snaking all down the fence.
Reckless beets, tiny, condensed in black wet –
its leaves are blood veins risen from dirt.

Flowers that never blossomed,
energy dispersed, delicate roots not thinned
between stunted plants and cellophane,
between a punctured ball and a worn glove.

This mistaken garden that still offers food,
that promises return for sun without cost,
that comes up for nothing out of the priceless earth,
that does not need me, that continues without the rake
and despite the greedy crows.

VET

I only knew one
who talked about it.
I pressed his bare thigh
with my palm, asked him
what Vietnam had been like.
He sat quietly a long time,
then told me this:
I was on guard duty
and I got bored so
I went out walking.
Came around a bend in the path
and there was this
VC shocked as I was
that we'd come face to face.
I don't know why
we just stood there like that
for what seemed the longest time
Then I shot him.

My lover smoked his cigarette.
What more do you want
to know?

We made love quickly
without kissing.
Sometime that night I heard
an eerie sound like a child

lost in a tunnel. I sat up
feeling the empty bed,
then went to get him where he was
crouched naked in the closet,
crying in his sleep, fists
clenched to his mouth.
I drew him to me
and led him back to bed,
unable to wake him.
He fell, then
into the silence of whatever ruin
he knew about
that I would remain apart from,
shaming and excluding him,
and we never
spoke of it again.

Question for the Newborn

Tell me once again exactly how it was
you grew yourself inside me cell by cell
after I made love to your father.
What it felt like to be two halves
suddenly whole in the dark world.
And even though you learned to sleep
through the night and put your fingers
in your mouth, if you think back
maybe it will come to you,
the ecstatic pain of cells dividing,
face coiling out of the brain,
the time in the mothery sea
when the outside of your face
was the same as your mind
and your skin was not a shell
but the inside of a flower
that in turn was a wound
so open we call it human.

MILK RITUAL

I look back from an older, calmer time
as the year I woke and woke
to lift him small and heavy
out of the crib to feed.
The year I saw his gray-blue head
skid out of me, wrinkled skull
strained to crowning.
Blue-black hair stung
from my final shudder
of muscle shoved.
My womb bit down hard
on his miraculous, finished body.
Lifeless, he hung, half-stuck,
not sure a body was the right place to be.
He slithered, limp,
separate, severed,
fallen out of the heavenly pulse.
No breath. Pale as rain sky.
Hands of the midwife wheeling
over his rose chest, tight bud,
chance of a heart and urgent
pull of air. Then
his cry sputtered
alone in the space that surrounded,
howled at the blue shock
of oxygen. She placed him
on my chest in a towel.

He glowed bruised pink,
sucked at my nipples
as evolution instructed.
Breathed in, drank in
light and world.
It was his need
against my sleep,
my self against his survival.
His every-three-hours cry
demanded that milky remembrance
of the warmth he'd cut from,
the summer I gave from my life
a second life
who stared back at me
with face familiar,
mysterious. The year
that love was hungry
and I fed it,
I fed it,
I fed it.

Past Life

Vague memory from a thousand years back.
I pole a wooden boat through mud water.
A river, black birds by clouds.
Suddenly a green moment.
I wake up from death.

I might have drowned, balance lost, water sucking me down.
Or a boulder-sized oxen fell on my working body.
Might have succumbed to a parasite that once grew
on a lily pad pecked by a white crane.

Can't remember if I was male
or female, though it mattered
terribly at the time. What I do know
is the moment when I took all I could
of my life at the moment it was gone.
Grabbed the green bamboo, the sound
of the stalks and feathers
pumping like breath as I passed
though the entire body
of the wind, out over the fading field.

There is only one second,
illuminated by shock,
even if you see death lounging
in your heart like an old friend
attending your illness.

But when it comes fast,
you take what you can
and sail in the direction
of everything splitting apart,
spinning until what's left of you
is everywhere and still connected
to your basket lying by the dirt path,
blue cloth wrapped over your former skin,
prepared for burning.

Is love out of reach then
and only earth? The birds say,
Look how absolutely nothing
holds us up and so we fly.
The whole flock turns,
one mind, knowing what?
And that was only
one of the lives I was blessed with.

Persephone's Ascent

What happened down here?
I hate to say it, but I fell in love.
What part of me was so harsh,
it stole me from the world of light?
Dragged me down here with my gauze dress
flailing in sunlight, my golden hair warning
the wind of my absence. I could blame
Pluto, as a man of his time – after all,
those sexy flames flowed from the pores
of his arms like a river of pilot lights.
Fire hallucinated around his legs and rose
up his thighs. Heat was anywhere in his body
there was wetness: his tongue and his eyes,
his semen even seared, a molten quality
that cooled when it found me.
In that cold underworld,
he had some need for relief and tenderness.
Were we to take our issues into therapy,
I could make him look terrible
as he was. But what I've learned
down here on the other side of the river Styx
in my interminable intimacy with him,
is that he is not a man,
but a god, as I am.
Other rules apply in the soul;
cure is not always so easy or desirable.

As I prepare to make my way back
to the surface of earth, my mother's home
with her bulbs pulsing under soil,
her ozone damp anxiety rushing rain
calling plants' chaos forth in honor of my return,
some voice in me must tell
what it is I came to love in my reign:
cavern, prison, entrapment, hole.
I was hidden down here for some reason
of sacred attention. In you, my human heart.
He and I, working it out in your
ruined life, or so, I know, it has seemed
to you after this body-dredged winter.
Look at the ravages on the surface since
I've been gone. My God.
I'm coming home.
Demeter will break the mean spell,
spill flowers out in celebration.
But hear me, oh human complexity,
heart and sore –
by coming down here for this length of time
I love you more. Spring is come.
I am risen, but I've promised to come back down.
My lack requires my presence.
Love the flowers, yes,
but don't depend on them. Smell them,
eat them, here, while I remind you why
I love the underworld as well.
I'm clear I live in two worlds
exactly the size of your life.

Saints and Fishing

"Prayer is not for the lazy. It is for those who, having worked diligently, will not tolerate defeat."
—George Santayana

The bait shop smelled of men and we inhaled aluminum, peered over moss-lined sides of the tank into the moving body of swarming shiners. Overhead on plywood-paneled walls hung totems of male significance: Day-Glo pink plastic night crawlers, lures and spinners, feathered with black-eye beads magically spun, jeweled fetishes with names like Lazy Ikes, Bass-O-Rino, June Bug Spinners, Daredevil. I was foreign and included, chewing Doublemint, wearing pink shorts, lucky to be among the powerful who knew they were down there in the deep, dying of old age: monstrous lunkers, ancient ones with rusted hooks still caught in their bony jaws. Down off the structure of sandbars they were waiting just like the meaning of life among the jellied seaweed and the ossified clamshells.

~

It was ritual more real than any church, my own father hierophant and keeper of the reels hung high on rafters, cane poles curved by sag of heat, stacked in the corner by the old piano, lines all tangled so that taking out just one involved a complicated litany of goddamn son of a bitch and jesus h christ who put these things away last fall?

~

The active form of prayer was in the training of the worms. He'd buy them at the bait shop, take them home to the pump room. In cheap Styrofoam ice chests of dry peat moss he set them loose, night crawlers oozing down into black soil. There in darkness they thirsted like supplicants. Meanwhile, Father waited on the moon. Seven hours after new moon on a windless evening; or was it twenty-four hours within the full moon just after a rain? No matter. He scooped out the worms, stuffed them into small containers, sponge-wet, and the worms, dehydrated, swelled, packed to the sides of the ice-cream box, pressed unmoving against the cardboard walls.

~

Clouds parted thin red gills over the water and out he set alone in the old battered speedboat with his Fish Lo-K-Tor, buzz of motor grinding the dusk rose light. Stumbling forward, he stood to drive, the boat planed out on the pearled lake. I watched him go, his silhouette against the perfect sun. Moths came in from the woods to bang the screens. The old stand-up radio with the green eye crackled Elvis and Patsy Cline out of Aitkin, KLIZ: "Look, look, my heart is an open book, I love nobody but you." The heat released a smell of mud and imminent rain and we forgot to pray.

~

We leapt out of top bunks, slammed outdoors and down the root path to the beach where he was shouting, "Lunker! Walleye! Ten pounds at least!" We stood there in seersucker nightgowns slapping mosquitoes while the huge arm of the fish was hauled on a stringer from the murk of night. It flapped once, muscular and dying, flailed against our father's wet shirt while he shouted about how he almost fell of the edge of the goddamn boat. "And on a night crawlers! God, yes, the succulent bastards! Those old ones are smart," he scowled, leaning toward us. "They won't bite at a piece of metal. They want something juicy, fat, squirming, delicious!" And we screamed, tore back up to the yellow eye of the cabin. He ran behind us, holding the thing aloft, slammed it into a pail so it wouldn't lose moisture, rammed out the dirt road in the station wagon to the Ideal Bar where they weighed the thing, snapped him with a Polaroid for the eternity of color film, his hand in its jaw, proper grimace, eyes half-closed from the flash. In the morning, there was the smell of butter, the snap-fizz of the fish in the black pan, black coffee, sun splashing all over the table.

~

The next night it was the same. Or dawn, foggy, already hot, depending on the moon. All that summer and summers I grew past old jack pines into hormones and my own obsessions, he was out there dragging the delicious water-logged bait prepared with loving cruelty to entice the great ones out of the deep. Oh, the belief we must have to call the fish from the watery depths. Patience, right angle of moon and proper bait. Boat rocking under fathomless stars, one mind silent on the lake of possibility. Oh, the feast that follows in the wake of such belief.

BASEMENT

I stand in the basement,
folding towels. They don't match:
frayed beach towels, so grey
they hardly absorb any water at all.
Chlorine smell of day-old socks
not transferred to the dryer.
Children asleep in deep rooms,
the flattened carpet
stained where the hot water heater
drained last Christmas Eve.

This week a bird flew down
the furnace chimney.
We cracked a window,
but it didn't fly out.
We put bread on the sill.
Sun and wind so close!
But it would not come to feed
at the edge of air. For some reason,
the dumb thing stayed down there with us,
unable to see the opening.

Sightseeing

North Shore, Lake Superior

I wonder what my children see
at the Split Rock Lighthouse.
White tiled military bricks.
In the keeper's house, the woodstove stoked by the wife.
Shortbread, glass bottles in the pantry.

I see the loneliness and isolation of her kitchen,
his view from the lighthouse over the slate lake.
But what do they see, those three in wet sneakers
and torn jeans galloping off marked trails, yelling
up into poplar branches, scaling beyond reach
of the terse sign: *No Rock Climbing Past This Point.*

I see the dynamited tunnel that made the first road
north of Duluth. I see how quiet it once was here,
before the stream of sullen families with their mini-cams
aimed at the horizon. But what do the children see,
leaping down the paved path to the water
at the ragged shore? They see feet in cold water,
flat skipping stones, they fall from a slippery rock and cry,
they want sticks to throw, they shimmy up a cliff,
stuck there, hollering back, laughing
for my camera: Look! We're up here
in the world where there's no history!

Looking the Other Way

Driving north in heat through cornfields,
I pass the nuclear plant at Monticello.
Giant sprinklers erected like insects in high green.
The beautiful tomatoes of Norm's vegetable stand
near the crackling power lines.
In joy, being out of the city
on a sudden day in summer,
I stop for cucumbers, fresh watermelon,
gold teeth of smiling corn,
grown in fields irrigated by the waters of the Mississippi,
the river that runs down to the city,
the city downstream from the power plant,
the power that fuels our light bulbs,
our music, our cooking.
I pile ripe food in a brown bag,
arms full of bulging fruit,
a song on my lips in the blue day,
and do not turn toward the steam rising cloudlike,
floating hugely south,
the sparkling pin-point lights on the reactor
in the center of the green corn of the nation,
the two tall towers of the nuclear plant
growing in the sky of our earth
near the headwaters of our one great river.

GLASS OF MILK

No poem can ever hold a gun
to the head of the human world,
no poem die
for the world to live.
Therefore it is important
to pour a glass of milk,
hold it carefully in two hands,
give it to a child to drink before bed
though there is no image
or statement to be made
and the floor is sometimes cold.

Coast of Gold

And when you get there,
do you check into paradise?

Yes, but down by the pool, a man's voice over a loudspeaker
shouts out bingo numbers, and the sun is so dazzling
that my numbers whiz up the coast with a squadron of pelicans.

And do you win the prize?

No, because when my card is nearly full of shells,
the man's voice over the loudspeaker yells out numbers
for a water aerobics class where women float
like oversized shrimp. Lift your arms! Uno, dos, tres,
cuatro, cinco, seis! Uno, dos, tres!

And over there, not fifty feet away in paradise, a man's voice
calls to the heaven within this heaven, waving a green flag
to the parasailer miles above all trouble,
but she does not hear him nor see the flag,
because in paradise you never come down.

The man hollers over the sound of a worker's hammer
on broken tiles as he chinks out corroded cement,
endlessly attempting to make repairs, forgetting that, here,
there is nothing that can be fixed. At last the world, as it is,
has become perfectamente, excelente, magnífico.

But when you reach for a glass of water, it dissolves
into sugar in your hand. You were thirsty,
but there is no thirst here, so you cannot drink.
When you reach for the sunburned arm of your lover,
to tell him how much you want him, he does not feel you,
because, here, there is no desire, no questions,
no aching, no actual limes.

Where in the world? you wonder. And then your search begins.
You will find your way back to earth if it kills you.

II

THE PRACTICE

THE GUIDE
Taos Pueblo Stables

The one in me who is unhappy
is angry at the sacred mountain,
blue in the thunderstorm,
lightning out over the mesa.
She doesn't want the sage smell after rain, sweet in her face.
She doesn't want the red horse catching the storm in his mane,
then blasting suddenly over the arroyo
and cantering fast over rocks.
When the mountain goes into her chest,
the horse drinks at the thin creek.

Her guide, Floyd, young, bare-chested,
waist-length black hair
blowing from under his baseball cap,
says, "I hunted rabbit here as a boy."
She asks him how old he was
when he was first on a pony.
"Three days," he says.
"How long have you worked here?" she asks.
"Summers," he says. "Before I head back to Princeton."
He takes off running toward the thin moon,
Taos lights blinking below.

She wants to scream,
Don't come in my breathing.
Love has broken the air in my body
and without that meaning, I won't know the way.

Rain now and the horse follows the guide
toward the steep embankment. She grips
leather reins, facing the end of the path:
two-hundred foot drop down into black lichen boulders.
He turns and laughs at her. "You didn't think
I'd lead you down there, did you?"

On the fast road back to the corral,
the horse takes her at his speed.
There are many kinds of weather all at the same time.
She forgets the story that brought her,
holding hard with her thighs
and bending toward the storm.

SANCTUARY

El Santuario de Chimayó, New Mexico

I went to El Santuario de Chimayó on a noon in April.
Lilacs flared lavender next to the crumbling adobe.

I drove in Eddie's car from Santa Fe, lonely on the road
that seemed a black lick over moon-red land.

I stopped in the dust to watch the light swim
the emptiness, a strip of sun sure as the mind of God,

proof in the blue distance. I went alone
to the small chapel at the edge of town.

The curio shop near the gravel parking lot
sold votive candles, rosaries in plastic eggs,

bookmark saints, shiny and amazing. I bought
a white candle and a souvenir egg to gather the sacred dirt,

said to bring miracles. Inside, the pews flicked
with busy grief. Votive flames leaned first to the left of Mary,

then to the right of Jesus, first this wooden Jesus,
lamb of affection, then that Jesus, bloody

in thorn crown agony, eyes bent up, feet dripping.
How many Jesus Christ Our Lords,

plaster, wooden, golden, glass, adorned the circus altar?
I sat on the hard bench. I'd never been religious,

never tasted a wafer, but I'd touched my own blood.
Tasted it. Did I have permission to pray?

Would the lotus, the rose, the blood, the lily, the soothing answer
be a place I could never go? I did not bend my head.

I'd left you days before. You'd come to me available
as water. You'd come white-fleshed and naked,

presenting your tongue to me, your wide chest,
your cracked hands. Both of us wore medals of failed marriages.

Mine was more recent. Yours was blacker, burned to ash,
while mine was a fresh flower pinned to my breast,

throbbing, blossoming. Your love came so easily
it was like drowning. You could breathe underwater,

you took me down with you. I couldn't swim or breathe.
My weight was heavy, the pure, round stone of fear.

I would be damned if I would love again. I rose from the pew,
went to the candles. I lit the match, said your name, and prayed

to understand the simplicity of change, the lurid crucifixion.
I wondered how long I would keep on dying. It was Sunday.

The plastic egg in my hand broke open, cheap beads in my palm.
I collected sacred dirt from the hole in the floor,

dipped it on my wrist like perfume,
and walked out over the red sand.

Outside, crows pecked for thrown bread. Holding hands,
families crossed the shallow river behind the church.

THE PRACTICE

There is that music
you used to hear
walking to the bus stop
in Boston each day.
It was always gray
the year you were young
out of that first bad marriage.
Seagulls circled clouds
over brick Italian streets
and you never believed the ocean was near
or escape possible.
Every morning you'd hear
from the upstairs window
of the three-story tenement
the saxophone's halting
hesitant scales
building up through that winter
of wet boots, cold sex,
unseen breath
blowing *Stormy Weather*
angelic
human fingers pressing
breath-stop holes
God Bless The Child
and other old jazz tunes
you knew the names to.
Walking that street

to the end each day
with an empty bag
to an empty room.
Loneliness was a luxury
with a name that wasn't yours
and a face you'd forgotten to love.
You'd rise early,
dress in a thin wool coat,
walk out hearing
that beginning golden music,
only practicing, only
practicing that one pure note,
that one breath, that one white bird
that would save you.

Life Everlasting

I want to hold on to this time
before it gets lost
out of some greed
that has to do with dying.
If I can just save
this one leaf,
thin ribbed jewel on the cement sidewalk,
as I step into its sun
and stand there,
die there,
resurrected next step
by the smell of the screen door,
old rust wire
on a Monday morning street.
I am born into the sadness
of the porch closed down for winter.
Dust on the floor, broth light.
I want to sit in the empty swing
in the shadow of the uneven vine.
I never want the door to close.

DRAFT CARD BURNING, 1968

For my brother

Burning your fingers,
you held that registration of soul,
refusing to go to execution in a small, wet country.
Hung an American flag upside down
on a black wall in your bedroom.
Drew cartoons for underground papers.
Staying up nights in speed frenzy,
drumming to a music no one else could hear,
you questioned, under it all,
deep in the leathery, masculine heart:
even so – coward – you told yourself.

Our father had been a Navy lieutenant
in a white midshipman's uniform.
A picture of the destroyer on his office wall
reminded him of days spent
sweeping minefields off Kyushu,
an island off the coast of Japan.
Our mother, a medic in the Women's Army Corps,
unwrapped putrid gauze from soldiers' dried wounds
fresh from the Pacific Theater.

Years later, you told me,
after you'd joined the army – Nam long over –
stateside, Fort Sill, Oklahoma,
after you'd become an expert marksman,

sharp-shooter, trophy winner, erasing,
in your fine service record, all those years
of drugs, lost jobs, bad debts,
why you held that card in flames
in front of the Federal Building:
Not some great politics at all. Prison
and a record were far preferable
to a plane depositing you in Hue,
Saigon, Da Nang. Still, all this time,
the shame you felt
in the gnawed pit of your life,
a male fear of dying.
We talked as you sat cleaning your prized gun,
taking care to make sure the safety was on.

Note: After reading this poem, my brother penciled in,
"Every man thinks meanly of himself for not having been a soldier."
—Samuel Johnson

Weapons

Even at two, my son shoots.
A stick, an oddly shaped rock
is a weapon.

After morning cartoons
comes *All Star Wrestling*.
Three boys stripped
to their underwear
hurt each other,
throw each other
to the carpet.
Then cry to the kitchen
for kisses, but by then
I'm angry at fighting.
Go figure out your own war.
I don't want to be the soother,
the balm mother who sorts and fixes.

Go to your room,
I tell them. Until
you figure it out for yourself.

I turn off the television.
Saturday is shining.
Their father will come
in an hour, for visitation.

If he decides to.

Pink Walls with Paintings

Georgia O'Keefe Museum, Santa Fe

Where the land curves down,
you don't know where you live.
Black doorway in adobe
or the way bones curve like music.
You don't know where you live
in your mind of traffic without color
until you see corn furl sunward
streaming, your life
in your luminous face.

⁓

A tendency toward exaltation
in the way her pale daylight moon
floats inside a hole
in a pelvis bone. She said
*The bones do not symbolize
death.* She liked the shapes.
Trace your eye along pastel
where there are no edges.
Know color and your eyes
are in love.

⁓

How to look closely
at a white rose: First see
where darkness steps forward
allow petals to form.
You don't need the whole rose

inside the frame. The flower
continues off the canvas,
outside the museum,
over the blue mountains.
It resides without ending.
The next painting is a petunia.

~

Words, she said, *do not*
describe as well as shapes.
Words fail, the heart grasps,
clinging to the violet
in the petunia, which is not,
after all, a real flower,
but a calling.

~

Each painting on the gallery wall
is not a flat surface of brush and pallet,
but a portal. Light vibrates the cornea.
You fall in and in
to the other brain,
the one you have not
spoken to in years.

~

Why do something
you don't want to do?
said the yellow sky.

Blue II, 1958. Corn II, 1924. Calla Lily Turned Away, 1923. Red Hills with Pedernal,
1936. Horses Skull with White Rose, 1931. Patio Door with Green Leaves, 1956.
Abstraction, White Rose, 1927. My Last Door, 1954. Black Place III, 1944. Pelvis Series,
Red with Yellow, 1945. Pelvis IV, 1944 (Moon).

APPETITE

Come down through hours of sage,
deserted towns, Southern Colorado, Northern New Mexico.
Down to the emptiness at the bottom of the country.
Come walk on the mesa, place your feet
in red powdered dust between the pinion
and the prickly pear cactus.
How long does it take to eat the end of love?
It doesn't end. You eat it
the way it rotted into a foul thing, the love still there,
of course. That's what made you so sick.
You ate the dead part of a living thing.
You can't live off that.

BEAUTY, 1963

Late night, transistor radio under my pillow so I can catch the station out of Chicago, tunes floating up to Minneapolis on damp Midwestern airwaves. It's Hot Forty, my curlers are orange juice cans, my hair slicked down with Dep, strands crackling dry into smooth curves, the torture of clips in my scalp. My cheeks are tight with dotted Clearasil. I feel my new breasts, those tiny walnuts, just barely tumors of womanhood in my white skin.

Pressed close to the bed, I'm craning to hear The Supremes in shimmering sequin gowns and helmet hairdos. Wearing my lace nightgown, my nails are Tango Pink. Don't chip it, don't flake the thumbnail, turn the radio down so Mom won't hear, hide the dancing, hide the bra she won't yet allow, nylons rolled up and stuffed in so I'll look bigger.

They're crying, "Stop in the name of Love," and I'm dreaming of cherry Cokes at Snyder's Drugstore, Noxzema, Maybelline, 45's, those flat black discs in a stack. Singing, "Blue, baby blue, I'm as blue as I can be," lying there in my blue bedroom, trying to disguise myself into beauty, not knowing even then how painful it was going to be.

Day After Vernal Equinox

Black snow leans by the back of the house,
smells like dead fish.
Dirt from city sky,
industry drifts amid sparse crystals.
The fallen world melts down into garbage.

Underneath—there it is!
The children yell, "Grass!"
They gaze down at the smashed odd green of it,
coming back into life only one day out of snow-melt.
I see a tangle of spilled noodles from a torn trash bag,
the yard littered with dog bones,
shredded newspapers blown against the fence.
Hesitantly, I acknowledge the difficult,
the old fence of my marriage and the oppressive sky.

But the children bend down over the ice
and the one open patch of grass.
They see it, blades emerging,
still pressed flat against sod-bed,
root-growth. They see the one thing,
the possible, and, announcing sun,
they begin to dance and shout
among the scattered clouds.

GHOSTS

In the years that followed
my twelve years with one man,
another opened my body
and told me there was more
to love than what I knew.
He told me to say the names
of his body as I touched him
in soft places in my mouth
or brought him hard to enter
with my fingers. I said
the names of my own body
and he laughed often and kept
the lights on. But afterwards
I would remember the strength
and timing of my old love,
how sex was the name
of my heart at its core where nothing
was held back. My new
lover liked to wash me
in the shower before tasting. We ate
the soap, the water in our hair.
But I stayed married to the ghost
and never spoke his name
in the sweetness afterward.
And for some reason
my lover slept far
to the edge of the bed,
not holding me in sleep,
and tearing the rose sheets
off the corner of the striped mattress.

First Prayer, Eight Years Old

I prayed for crayons in that icy bedroom.
Diamond-patterned curtains,
multicolored with black dots.
The white dark came right up to the house,
air so cold it cracked. I stood
on my pillow peering out the window,
wanting that box of 64 Crayolas
with the sharpener in the back.
I said the names: magenta,
umber, burnt sienna.
I did not have any idea of God,
but a star seemed good.
The far other. I didn't know
the asking itself
was God for the moment.
Not having something longed for,
I sucked the words in my mind:
Scarlet. Hyacinth.
I wanted perfection. I reached
into the snow for it
and got nothing instead,
a better beginning,
the make-do, empty page.

Café, Taos

White plastic chairs under the arbor in the shade.
The morning is mountain dusty.
Hollyhocks against the adobe wall of the bookstore.
Taos crowded with tourists.
They stand at the crosswalk in the bright air.
Couples look odd, tired from driving, not used
to so much time together.
But another couple in the Caffé Tazza
reads the newspaper together quietly.
I imagine they made love this morning in their room.
Her thighs are milky and fleshy, but her waist is thin.
They are in their forties, graying.
The man's legs are muscular and tan.
They are speaking German.
She is almost singing to the quiet hum of the street
over the adobe wall where a mop is leaning.
I imagine she surprised him
by grabbing him in sleep under the comforter.
Kneading him hard and climbing on him
with her small breasts and breadlike, loaflike thighs
splitting open the moist nutrition of her love.
I can't imagine loving in that comfort.
Before they leave, he digs in her purse
for the camera. She smiles, delighted,
her teeth slightly buck. He is almost handsome.
She is almost homely. He licks the jam
off her fingers and she snaps him

by the blue door. Maybe they have grown children,
like their jobs, and enjoy traveling together.
I watch love in the café as if I am studying a foreign species.
See how the bird calls in the tree. Now the patio is empty,
the gravel cool in shade.
The dogs have come begging and left.

Words Themselves

Words themselves,
black ink
on white paper - trees
died for this.

.

Words themselves discuss
their relationship:
pages pressed together
in a closed notebook.

.

Words themselves
don't care
how the story turns out.

MOTHER'S CROSSWORD, 1960

She props the folded newspaper in her lap,
brushes flies away. Daily crossword.
Dissector, collector of words like *irk* and *yen*,
words that name things unheard of:
cousin of Wordsworth, city on the Ganges.
Words in lines that intersect,
neat meaning, pattern perfect,
lightly penciled in. French for *quiet*,
Spanish for *room*. I want to call out to her
through the word *distance*,
beg for something to eat
in that silence she owns.

Later when gnats batter the lamp
over the dinner table, we sit facing each other.
Scrabble. All my letters
look like Vietnamese. Hawaiian. I can't spell
quixotic or even *yak* to make good points.
I don't add up. The moon rises
over her shoulder outside the screen.
Surely I am laughing as I click
the wooden squares around, searching
for just the right word on the terry tablecloth.
She spells out *creamy* – *Y* on the triple point.
I put down *on*. She puts down *oxen*.
I reach in the corduroy bag,
feeling for the one magic letter. Now

the board is full of words. It doesn't matter
that I've lost. I clamber up on the top bunk
in the damp night, Mother across the room
reading again, more words to fill in space,
to gather lives into that intense disc of light
on the page that is the real world.

Mother Hunger

I've been hungry for weeks,
odd times of day,
midmorning barbeque chicken,
late night desire for cream soup.
Empty mouth, hungry day.
Pile the plate, fill the pot,
pasta, potato, tomato puree.
I'm in charge of hunger
in this family. Mother's lot:
salt, flour, syrup spilled
on the pantry shelf.
It used to be only my own binge
or bulge, those grapefruit halves,
ten glasses of water or five-day fasts
on carrot juice til my hands
turned saffron in the sink.
Now they stare, my children
with upturned mouths
of birds while I promise,
plead: Eat what I've made.
Eat to be good. Good to eat.
Chew, spew, swallow your pride,
serve ABC Spaghettios.
No roast, wheat toast or homemade jam.
Not this mom, out of time
rushed in a scurry from the busy freeway.
After the free-for-all, throw

the scraps to the yowling cat,
collapse standing up to put away
rinsed plates, passed cups.
There's no hearth, just hurry.
Does it matter what the platter serves?
Nerves of the home
from the kitchen flow.
Go to bed tired of food,
feeding, dreaming suddenly
at 11:37 p.m. of an avocado
and turkey sandwich, a deviled egg,
a feast prepared
by anyone but me.

What Picasso Saw

The family's large moon faces,
raw masks carved big, curved,
bright primary colors
profile or full to the front:
red, yellow, blue. Always the odd
dislocation,
two eyes on same side of head,
lips beside the nose. Fathers loom,
mothers face the side and you're more drawn
to a round breast with a nipple
that sees like an eye
so that her sex is what you see in her.
I don't recall female children,
only a consistent son, fierce,
grinning devil, fiery green arms,
animal teeth. His penis
is a high-kicked leg,
fat phallus aiming at the viewer.

What strikes me is the truth of line.
The artist drew one stroke for the side
of mother's face; that same line
is father's shoulder.
A curve of nose defined in him
is also the edge of her arm
reaching through his forehead.
The son is below, his skull formed

by his father's leaning belly
pressing him down, but he rises anyway,
the strong child.
There is no separate mouth between the parents.
They share those black brick lips.
An ear comes twice off the same cheek.
That hand belongs to two.

Don't you see how he saw
how we cannot pull
away from the family's love
where there are no edges of self to own:
your mother's lips in your ear,
father's chest the top of your head.
But if you let your will beam,
strong solar plexus grin, bare teeth
at the base of the picture and shine,
you can say,
I am here. I am separate.
I am not your edges, mother, father,
husband, sons. I am going off now
to start my own painting.
I am the only one in it.
All the edges are mine.

THE TRIP

Two days left.
Already I'm sad to be going.
Missing the pinion,
cold cherry blossoms,
decaying adobe houses
on the road to Peñasco
where someone lived a whole life
or part of one.

Missing what you have
and still have more of –
dumb heart! You'll miss your death
two days before it happens.

III

TOURIST IN THE PURE LAND

Saturday Night at the Emporium of Jazz

For Jay McShann, Kansas City Blues Piano Man Extraordinaire

God, if there be a heaven
let it be Saturday night
at the Emporium of Jazz in Mendota,
Jay McShann in a shimmering brown suit,
his hands blurred reflections
in perfectly sheened ebony
of the piano. Smoke in air
dusky like half-rain
outside November night. Let it be
two hundred miles from the headwaters
of the Mississippi River. Let
St. Louis, Memphis, New Orleans
be in a long line beneath us
in America. And music
come off his big back,
lift off like wings of many birds
on a migratory river, stamping
water-surface flight. And let
three horns stand upright
at stage edge, silver cornet,
black clarinet, golden
tall trombone on the red
indoor-outdoor carpeting
of the low stage,

a fire extinguisher on the floor
next to the piano
for when the music gets hot
and a pile of spilled ice cubes
next to the piano bench,
melting in the pink spotlight.
Let there be clink of glasses
and loud voices back by the bar
so you get angry. Dear god,
let heaven be loud. Let there be
human anger in a white cloud.
Let music make you forget
the blood in your hands
that cannot stop patting
your knee and may Jay
McShann's whole body play,
not just hands but all ten
fingers a choir on keys
never before touched and then
touched in every way by a man
in a roadhouse bar in this
fog of a down-hearted country.
Let love be this clear and direct: *Baby,*
don't you want a man like me?
Let one glass be half full
of whiskey and the other
full of beer. *Baby, let me*
love you til my face turns cherry red.
Trains cross America in our minds,
pure as old jazz tuned

in broad backs bent to work
on a piece of metal, a hot stove,
back bent over a woman
in an unmade bed out of some longing
that skin can satisfy.
Let that song go out in this heaven,
Jay McShann at the baby grand.
Let earth be small, hot smoke,
full ashtray, dark on one side
of the river, music on the other,
while the last note lingers, growling
over the cold, cold water.

ZEN DEATHBED POEMS

Paradise murmurs underfoot.
Goodbye every breath.
Fireflies on black mountain.
Birds 5 a.m. wake me, crying.
I say crying. They say singing.

.

Two days rain
at Catching the Moon Monastery.
I had no idea
the bell would be so loud.

.

Hidden road, hidden view.
High weeds, new road.
Suddenly
I'm lost.

.

The last thing I thought was
that's it? But I'm
hungry.

.

White heron by my house.
I remembering seeing it,
white air, after
it's gone.

.

Was life so much
whining? I
meant to...
.

Swallow jag-tail
swooping over a fast truck.
Inside humans sing
So fine.
.

Black rain on Hokyoji Mountain.
Wherever you're going
stop.

THREE SUNS

Thank God for Garcia Lorca!
Only his voice still alive on the earth
tells me to put citrus fruit in a clay bowl
on the winter solstice.
Only his rivers thick with memory
make us believe we're immortal.

God of grocery stores, god of coins,
god of black watch on a wrist
and angel of rushing traffic,
be kind to our small bent bodies.
Tell us we'll be young again,
where love was trusted,
saved naked in the cool lake,
a pail of water outside the door,
the abandoned car behind the cabin.

Let us pray.
Let us not forget the many nameless
survivors of history
and that we are among them.
Even broke we are wealthy
flying in our minds in a country
where no one checks us at state borders.
Even broken we are healthy and sexual,
our bodies warm in the late day.

Isn't this a dream?
One brick of cheese on a cracked plate,
two cigarettes burning in our cherry lips,
three suns floating low over paradise:
one in our perfect memory,
one that will never come,
and this one here, the great one over us
by the bare trees shining.

At the Gateway

For my father

Before you die, I stand with you
at the gateway. As it widens.
As you lie in the blue sheets of the ICU,
as tubes enter your body at your wrists,
at your groin, at your mouth.
As oxygen breathes you, as red monitors
wave in crests and valleys
like a thought pattern.
I stand with you – conscious in your morphine stupor –
the life-widening emptiness open
and real as your name or mine
called across a field on a summer's day in childhood
through dragonflies, goldenrod, meadowlarks, grasshoppers
– *come home come home now before it is dark* –
but it is already dark. You do not want to come home.

When you float up out of drugged sleep,
your throat full of the ventilator tube,
your arms restrained, you can't speak,
but you tell me anyway with your old feisty anger at life
that neither do you want to stay, not like this.
So I stand with you at the gate, the opening
that is your heart. We listen to jazz on the CD
just under the monitor where your crazy pulse
is dancing, the nurse says. I feel you at that opening
in terror and acceptance, in the tide of relief and disgust.

Your whole being saying *oh all right, fuck it,*
and then *I'll always love you. I'll never leave you.*

When you do and I remain in your vibrant absence,
you sometimes greet me, close as my face
from the starlight over cold Midwestern streets.
I've heard somewhere stars are the eyes of god
but it is the blackness that is god
and you are the star of emptiness
over the smoking chimneys,
the State Fair water tower, and the places
on the snow where the streetlight shines
and on the places where it does not.

Key West: Ernest Hemingway's House

Things unto themselves are shining.
The red gloss of an old pickup truck
newly painted. The ghost of a dead writer
still standing at his desk
in heat overlooking the palm trees.
We don't care anymore about
your failed marriages, Ernest Hemingway.
The fights over money,
the blast to your brain
after drink downed you and words
did not come anymore. We don't remember
the sickness of particular nights. We see
something greater beyond
the house, past the patio, long past
Cuba, Sun Valley, past the earth
of our numbered days
where they are still living,
those words and others
with the ceramic cat by Picasso on the bureau.
There is something in our raving
we can leave to the green days
which outlasts our large unending sorrow,
our small beds and sunburned hands.

WHAT WE'VE COME TO

When I hear the old Beatles song
blare in the Croissant Express,
some part of me is confused
I've ended up here
with this cracked cup of coffee.
Some part of me
is still back in August of '69,
sitting on the roof finding the cosmic
in a yellow window,
leaves painting paisley in my liquid mind.
Part of me can't believe
we'd ever think so much
about the broken muffler.
That dinner would take precedence
over dancing. And it wouldn't be
a beautiful soup brewing in a cast iron pot,
it would be meat.
It would be chicken I cut myself,
washing the blood off the bones.

How You Go On

You take care of the things of this world.
Bury roses. Make a deep cut by the roots.
Angle the root-ball down.
Cover the whole stem with dirt,
layers of leaves against cold.

Do what you can
and then the next.
Dust piano.
Feed cat.

You keep remembering
and the remembering blows away,
a faded World War II snapshot,
end over end,
light fused behind the couple
(holding hands,
sometime after the wedding).

You watch your life
about to fall off the sheer edge
of the known,
but when you approach,
they pull you back,
mouthing in the silence:
You can't go there.
It's not so bad.
It's all right.
It's only this.
Bear it.

THE QUESTION ABOUT WOMEN

In a kitchen, of course, in a kitchen.
The question of corn oil burning in a bent pan.
The question of Sunday dinner after a hollow day in April,
of who's washing the dishes afterward downstairs
and the question upstairs of the children bathing,
the question of them being male.

The question of women and money, of needing
And not needing men, the average Dow Jones Average
language of power,
of women and their ability to reproduce
in their bodies and who then
owns the sons and the daughters.
Question of custody.

The historical importance of dinner,
early moments of bonding with the infant,
awake and alert at the end of the twentieth century,
the father faint in a green chair after he cut the cord.
How the sons have come of age
at the beginning of the twenty-first century
just in time for another money war.
The question of love being possible
at odd moments in the world.
Then impossible.

Question of underground missiles, North Dakota,
bare ground twisting away across
Ethiopia, Somalia, Sudan.

Skulls lined up in pits in Grenada, Bosnia.
Heartland soothe of rain on the Midwest city.
Are we too many insects
lacking a sense of our collective life?
The planet itself alive
and we some diseased micro-organism
earth might be trying throw off its jeweled skin?

The question of earth's arsenal an act against
the sexual drive, the ultimate failure
of testicles to produce hormones
in a garden of equal flowers.
Of men resisting the difficult feast of the family.
Daily as supper, vast as foreclosures.
Extreme tactics, persuadable voters.

Question of eggs
diving down fallopian tubes regardless of drought.
Lip on lip, wet tongues not speaking.
The failure of language to convince us
of the magnitude of secrets.
The question every day of food, of women,
of whether or not there is any more reality
to dinner than to anthrax.
Death being the larger force of real?

Or when April goes exploding again, not land mines
but the luxury of leaves.
Rain out of Canada, its level of acidity.
The question of the contamination of the known world,
this sadness of spirit we live with
and continue to love in spite of.

NOTATIONS: POOLSIDE

In this sacred
day's expanse
of dimpled thighs,
of plush, bikinied woman's
dragon-tattooed, ample breast,
an ink snake licking
down her melon-rounded knee
near the poinsettia border
near thatched grass
by the aqua filigreed pattern
of chlorine light, swung,
dallied, calligraphy in waves
wound concentric after
cannonball splash,
the dappled ease of
an arc-flown beach ball
over a sagging badminton net
through piña colada blare
of crooning, too-loud
blasting operatic techno
mariachi throngs of notes
rise high as gliding birds
that ride wind updrafting
cool through clouds
near the pink balcony
of the penthouse
of the Hotel del Oro.

HIBISCUS

Negril, Jamaica

A rooster crows, Sunday morning.
What are the wide flowers by the wood porch rail?
Last night, a pale lizard on the wall.
Why, even in beauty, remember lost
lovers and husbands
whose anger I had to leave?
I dream of those who did not please me,
and those to whom I could not open my gasping heart.

The flowers may be hibiscus.
Red ginger by the fence.
Poinciana trees, orange in blossom across the road.

I savor new words
on the tongue in my mind
where seeing goes deeper than vision
into a tasting, a digestion, a fucking of colors.
I am greedy in sex as I am older.
Order my man around: *Do this, touch this,*
turn over, look at me, don't look away.

From the hibiscus with its rippled labial petals
curled back in early heat,
the stamen droops straight out,
furred with minute coral hairs,
each with its own pollen ball at the tip

where a five-pronged star of deeper, pinker pink,
pink aching for pink, aches so hard
it becomes generous,
shoves pink out among the cooing of mourning doves.
One blossom spent
now drops to the first white rail of the porch.
Hunger is a gift. Life eats itself.

Letting Go

By the way,
the one who loved you those years?
She died.

Today I noticed
purple salvia
by the steps –
edges already rust
before the first sharp frost.

No one's fault.
Summer's over.

A box of daylilies
next to the house,
not yet planted.

There is still time.

Meditation Retreat in 12 Parts

On the Way
Anticipating lack,
I pack coffee to wake, shawl for cold,
cherry Tootsie Roll Pops for hunger.
Not enough
looms as we drive by wide water.

.

4:15 a.m.
White moon seen
twice through tent screen.
When the door unzips –
just one moon.

.

At Breakfast
Orange. Eating
the color.

.

Inhale
At first I can only breathe.
At last I can breathe.

.

Morning Bell.
Was it outside
or inside?
Birds sing all over
my body.

.

Realms
Sitting, I review
all past loves.
I see
they are past.

.

Mirror
Ah, Hungry Ghost!
My ex-husband –
Which one?

.

Not
If you think this is
a poem, you're
thinking.

.

Two Minds
I like myself
I don't like myself
I like myself
I don't like myself
I like the wind
I don't like the bug
I like the bug
I don't like the wind
Practice
non-preference

Teacher to Cook:
"Will you be here for the indefinite future?"
Cook to Teacher:
"I think so."

Indefinite future –
Oh, how I miss you.

.

Tornado Warning
Down in the zendo basement
storehouse consciousness,
thoughts rise as bouncing hail.
Thunder Sutra.
All ten directions!
Only two tents left standing –
impermanent homes
blown away.

.

The Way
In the field, a lake.
In the grass, a river.
Frog on no path.

TOURIST IN THE PURE LAND

All I know is that under my breathing,
I've stopped pushing it away.
If the Caribbean is so luminous in late June,
if the hibiscus falls damp on the stone walk,
it is good to know the words to dumb sweet songs.
I will sing them. I will notice the shadow
in fat moonlight by the black surf.

Of course, the travel writers I read at night in the villa
are right to chide me: I am white, it is the twenty-first century.
One faucet drips water in a ditch at dinner time
where women line up with buckets among wandering pigs.
The glass-bottom boat hovers over the wreckage
of a ganja plane, so far down in the sweet blue it looks like a toy,
dumped there on purpose to make an artificial reef,
something for us tourists to gaze down at.

So what if the boat needs a destination for the half-day tour?
I'll take that wreckage and the tin-roofed houses
and the chicken that pecks in the open door
while I cook. I'll take the fever
in the air-conditioned bedroom, the flour strike,
no bread for weeks, the tree
hung with purple orchids over the river.

I'm not going to turn down happiness anymore.
There is no pure moment untouched by poverty or capitalism.
Nothing is going to stop me
from wading in salt water, bare-breasted,
one hundred yards down from Alvin's fruit stand –
pineapple, plantain, no problem.
If I don't love now, it will have to be from choice.
And if my heart can't take goodness, it can stay dreaming
of every old love out of reach. That will keep it busy
while I grate fresh coconut, drain its thin milk
in the battered saucepan, add red beans,
and, later, rice.

MANATEE AND PELICAN

Where is poetry?
It's around here somewhere.
A giant manatee cruises under the walking bridge
on the Florida island, a dark mammoth thing,
graceful in its green element,
somehow able to live among the boat slips
and the condo developments.

The ease of the pelican
scooping schools of silvery fish,
a moment of holding the water
in its brown sack of a beak,
then gulping it all down while a seagull
sits on its head, friendly, waiting for a tidbit
to drop out.

But another pelican snags
a fisherman's hook and bait and line
in its deep gullet and the man catches him,
tries to hold the massive wings in his arms,
salty, wet, the strength in the flapping wings,
the thing in its throat. He tries to close
the pelican's beak with his hand, feeling
how it is all caught somewhere.

Boys gather on the dock to watch the drama briefly,
while out in the Gulf somewhere,
a swirl of dead water coagulates,
fertilizer run-off, sewage, industrial dumpage,
detritus of the beautiful mansions by the sea.

I could no longer watch the man
struggle with the bird, though it was clear
the man was kindly at heart and loved the sea.
The lure would be gotten out
of the tear in pelican's gullet or tongue or
inner slime of its beak
and eventually the bird would bob again,
sore, healing. It would swallow
in the feeding and floating
that is its life.

ABOUT THE AUTHOR

For Kate Green's previous collections of poems, *The Bell in the Silent Body* and *If the World is Running Out*, she was awarded two Bush Foundation Fellowships in Poetry and a Loft McKnight Award. Her novel *Shattered Moon*, was nominated for the Edgar Allan Poe Award and was a Book-of-the-Month Club Selection. She has published four other mystery novels, several of which have been optioned for films. *Shattered Moon, Night Angel, Shooting Star, Black Dreams*, and *Fallen Angel* were published in over ten foreign languages. *Black Dreams* won the Minnesota Book Award. She has also written eight books for children, including *A Number of Animals* (co-written with Christopher Wormell who also illustrated the book); it was selected as a *New York Times* Best Illustrated Book of the Year. She lives right across from the Minnesota State Fairgrounds in St. Paul, and teaches writing and literature at North Hennepin Community College in Minneapolis, Minnesota.

Please visit her website, *www.kategreenwrites.com*